Becoming the Light

Copyright © 2021 by Serenity G. Amerson

Printed in the United States of America
Becoming the Light

ISBN 9798487585592
Published by Poitier Wordsmith Academy

Becoming the Light

WRITTEN BY
SERENITY G. AMERSON

A DEVOTIONAL FOR TEENS

Becoming the Light

Serenity G. Amerson has a passion for encouraging and inspiring youth of all ages. Her passion is to help other children just like her, cope with childhood depression, insecurities, overcoming his/her/they disabilities, and encouraging youth to shine their lights bright so that the entire world can see how awesome and special he/she/they are.

She wants all children to know that they are not alone in this world, and not matter how tough things may seem, they will get through it as long as they believe in themselves and remember that each of them are valued, special, and an important factor in this world.

The Introduction

This devotional is all about Becoming the Light. It is a story that highlights events in the upbringing of a sixteen-year-old named, Serenity G. Amerson whose experiences led her to see the Light of God. Once she was able to embrace the light, her entire future changed!

Becoming the Light contains several life lessons as well as crucial advice, from the point-of-view of a teenager growing up within the 2000's: otherwise known as, "Gen-Z." This is my contribution to you, motivating you to persevere as I wish to inspire confidence within you. I want to let you know that you can live your purpose if you walk in God's plan and put in the work, despite life's obstacles.

Hopefully, within these pages, you will come to understand my journey and how I became who I am today. These testimonials are meant to help you with any emotion(s) or situation(s) that you may feel and further allow you to relate to each one.

I have included lines in this devotional to give you an opportunity to start your journey to Becoming the Light within your own circles. Pour out your heart, ideas, and emotions onto these pages and when you feel you are losing your way, need encouragement, or want to smile about where God has taken you... go back to your documented love!

Thank you so much for taking the time to read this Devotional.

I promise it will change your life, if you let it! I wish you the best.

Becoming the Light

Day 1... The Beginning

The day was August 14th, 2005, a momentous day. At a small, Plantation hospital in South Florida, a little monster was born (something my mother decided to call me)! However, this little monster had no idea that it would be the beginning of a fight that she would have to endure her entire life. I was only five pounds and one ounce, because I was born one month early, due to health issues. I was given the name, Serenity Gabriel Amerson, chosen by my beautiful mother, Brittany Poitier. My mom was young and vibrant, yet inexperienced when she had me. Though she knew it was not going to be easy, she knew that it would be worth it. Each time she looked into my eyes she saw the light God had shared with her and she vowed that she would share it with me, so that one day, I too could share my light with you!

Becoming the Light

Scripture

_____

_____

_____

Devotional

_____

_____

_____

_____

_____

_____

_____

_____

_____

_____

_____

_____

_____

_____

_____

_____

_____

_____

_____

_____

Becoming the Light

Day 2... The Storm

      In 2005, a category five hurricane, Hurricane Wilma, hit the area a week after I was born, destroying our entire apartment and causing us to have to start over... literally. Though my mother was a new mom with various challenges, she rolled up her sleeves and went to work, restoring our lives. In a few months, my mom had gotten everything back in order and was soon blessed with an addition to our family, despite the loss and struggle. Through times of despair, frustration, and feelings of hopelessness, my mother held on to the light of Christ, praying and receiving good counsel as He shone a way to our recovery. When we encounter the storm, we must continue to move forward. Yes, we need cover, but as we pray and ask God for that covering, we must keep moving forward until we see signs that we are Becoming the Light. That is where our hope always lies. In God, using our lives to shine light on HIM!

Becoming the Light

Scripture

_____
_____
_____

Devotional

_____
_____
_____
_____
_____
_____
_____
_____
_____
_____
_____
_____
_____
_____
_____
_____
_____
_____
_____
_____

Becoming the Light

Day 3... Sion is Here!

As soon as I could talk, I would beg momma every day for a little brother. Finally, the moment had arrived and I was so excited. From then on, I learned that even in the middle of new beginnings, you can be blessed, using that strength gained in struggle to shed light on future obstacles.

Momma gave birth to my brother in 2007, but a few months later, we realized there was something different about my brother, Sion. After endless questions, tests, and research, we discovered that he had Autism. My mother went ahead and looked into some things after being told that we had to change our whole life around for Sion's special needs. As of now, it has been hard having a brother that does not process things the way I do, or function the way I do, so it took some getting used to. On the other hand, I had some demons of my own to fight, so it made me more sympathetic towards Sion.

At the age of six, I was diagnosed with Dyslexia and A.D.H.D. Attention Deficit Hyperactive Disorder. It was hard learning to read and do most of the things that all the other kids were easily able to do. This is the major reason as to why I was held back in the third grade. These learning issues affected how I took my state test and therefore, I was held back. Some kids would have spun out of control, but for me, it gave me a story to tell and the light to see how hard it was for Sion. Now, I am part of many Autism Awareness drives as well as other events, helping me Become a Light for those who are being eaten up by their difficult lives.

Becoming the Light

Scripture

_____
_____
_____

Devotional

_____
_____
_____
_____
_____
_____
_____
_____
_____
_____
_____
_____
_____
_____
_____
_____
_____
_____
_____
_____
_____

Becoming the Light

Day 4... The Teachers' Contributions

My teachers always told me that I was unteachable. They assumed that because I did not have a father in my life, I lacked a guiding, parental figure. Teachers can be a light to their students, but in this case, my teachers made me feel like I could not do or be anyone worthwhile. Thankfully, my saving grace was my mom. Despite having us, she was determined to finish college. She would always say, quoting the words of William James, "Act as if what you do makes a difference. It does." Whenever I felt like I could not learn, those words filled me with enough courage to keep going. I almost failed this stage of my Becoming the Light because I could not count on the world to see me through. Now, with everything that is going on, I know where my help comes from, and that is The Light... God! It has made me into the strong learner I am today.

Becoming the Light

Scripture

_____
_____
_____

Devotional

_____
_____
_____
_____
_____
_____
_____
_____
_____
_____
_____
_____
_____
_____
_____
_____
_____
_____
_____
_____
_____
_____

Becoming the Light

Day 5... The Mental

I battle depression just like my mother. We both got bullied in grade school, and it continued for me in high school. The kids told me that I was the reason I had learning issues and tried to make me feel like I was less of a person because of it. Millions of people suffer with Dyslexia and A.D.H.D, but during that time, I felt like I was the only one.

I used social media as my 'get away', a way to escape the negative remarks. Unfortunately, it just made everything worse. I began acting different, dressing different, and even changed the way I ate, just so I could be like the other kids and have them accept me. My mom tried to tell me that it would not work, but like most teenagers, it went in one ear and out the other. She didn't know how I felt, and she was too old to remember how hard It was growing up surrounded by people who make you feel worthless. She was already a light; she was not struggling to become one. Little did I know, we all struggle with Becoming the Light, and just because we have aged, does not mean our struggle is over. Becoming the Light is a life journey!

Becoming the Light

Scripture

_____
_____
_____

Devotional

_____
_____
_____
_____
_____
_____
_____
_____
_____
_____
_____
_____
_____
_____
_____
_____
_____
_____
_____

Becoming the Light

Day 6... The Insecurity of it All...

I soon became insecure about myself because I did not look like most girls on Facebook, Instagram, or TikTok. The depression became too much for me to handle and the insecurities were out of control. It took a lot of mentoring and my mom talking in my ear, for me to finally understand that I am beautiful just the way I am. She told me not to fall into the wrong crowd by trying to fit in, instead she told me that I needed to be a leader! This is where Becoming the Light came from.

Every time I got in trouble or after a deep discussion with my mom, she would say, "Serenity, you need to be the light!"

If I am the light that leads people to God, I can't let my depression and insecurities take over. Those issues must be destroyed by my walk! Becoming the Light changed everything...

Becoming the Light

Scripture

_____
_____
_____

Devotional

_____
_____
_____
_____
_____
_____
_____
_____
_____
_____
_____
_____
_____
_____
_____
_____
_____
_____
_____
_____
_____
_____

Becoming the Light

Day 7... Eye Opening

I really started opening my eyes after I found out that the path I was headed for wasn't a great one. Parents and school counselors spend hours trying to convince us to stop messing up our own lives with the poor choices that we make. They assume it is because we are "in our feelings." So, I changed myself...again. I started being antisocial, so that I would not follow the wrong crowd and mess myself up before I even graduated. As we walk, we reach levels on our path to purpose, and those levels lead us to either success or failure. Becoming the Light helps us direct those who get lost along the way, ensuring that we stay on the right path together!

Becoming the Light

Scripture

_____
_____
_____

Devotional

_____
_____
_____
_____
_____
_____
_____
_____
_____
_____
_____
_____
_____
_____
_____
_____
_____
_____
_____
_____
_____

Becoming the Light

Day 8... The Work

After a lot of work, process, and improving, I am standing here today about to graduate at the age of sixteen! Even through all the setbacks and bumps along the way, no matter how bad or how complicated a situation can be: from an absence of a parent, mind-numbing depression, or chaotic insecurities, you have got to push through it to get to where you want to be. It was Exodus 14:14 from the Holy Bible that did it for me, and I can testify today because I held on to these words!

"The Lord will fight for you; you need only to be still."

Becoming the Light has caused me to make better decisions and has helped me understand why I am here. When you know that you have a purpose, it can get you through many rough patches. We have no control over some things in life, but we can control our own light!

Becoming the Light

Scripture

_____
_____
_____

Devotional

_____
_____
_____
_____
_____
_____
_____
_____
_____
_____
_____
_____
_____
_____
_____
_____
_____
_____
_____
_____
_____

Becoming the Light

Day 9... The Role Model

My biggest role model is my mom! She has had three kids and a lot of setbacks in her life, but each time, she pushed any negative thoughts behind her and did not let anything come between her and her success. She is raising the three of us with love and some support, opening our eyes and teaching us to share our light, despite obstacles!

Today, she is one of the only African American women in the N.H.R.A. National Hot Rod Association, and the I.H.R.A. International Hot Rod Association. She has also graduated with her master's degree, with a plan to earn her doctorate in August. Being included in her journey, and keeping my eyes on her, has shown me that Becoming the Light is something I too can do if I follow God's plan. We all have a part to play in the kingdom, and sharing my story allows others to be inspired, just as my mom inspires me!

Becoming the Light

Scripture

_____

_____

_____

Devotional

_____

_____

_____

_____

_____

_____

_____

_____

_____

_____

_____

_____

_____

_____

_____

_____

_____

_____

_____

_____

_____

Becoming the Light

Day 10... The Journey...Present!

Everything I do and achieve is because my mom has motivated me to do my part and I want to do it not just for me but for her as well. She has sacrificed so much for our family and I want her to know I hear her!

God is counting on each of us to share our trials, our victories, and our ability to make it through. If I can do it, then my light proves that you can too. Every day I rise from sleep, I promise to always be the light I was put on this earth to be. It is my wish again, that something in this devotional has led you to Becoming the Light for those God places in your path to help!

Becoming the Light

Scripture

_____

_____

_____

Devotional

_____

_____

_____

_____

_____

_____

_____

_____

_____

_____

_____

_____

_____

_____

_____

_____

_____

_____

_____

_____

_____

Made in the USA
Middletown, DE
22 October 2021